To: Mr. Kinney

[signature]
'2019'

*- Thank you for reading
My Story.
Be Blessed...*

UnEqually Yoked...

" I do, I did &I don't"

THE STORY OF MY MARRIAGE AND HOW GOD KEPT ME

& A Personal Journal at the end of book

Written By: Lorinda Macon

Copyright © 2019 by Lorinda Macon

All rights reserved.
This book or parts thereof may not be reproduced in any form, stored in any retrieval system, or transmitted in any form by any means—electronic, mechanical, photocopy, recording, or otherwise—without prior written permission of the publisher, except as provided by United States of America copyright law.

Cover photo credit: Lorinda Macon

The opinions expressed in this manuscript are solely the opinions of the author and do not represent the opinions or thoughts of the publisher. The author has represented and wanted full ownership and/or legal right to publish all the materials in this book.

ISBN 978-1-79470-711-5

PRINTED IN THE UNITED STATES OF AMERICA

After getting married in the eyes of God
the two becomes one...
One Mind, One Body & One Soul.

According to the Holy Bible...
Marriage is said to be a Holy Covenant before God!

Table of Contents

Dedication

Special Thanks

To My Spiritual Parents and Church Family

Foreword

Spoken Word

UnEqually Yoked

A formed Covenant

Introduction

Marriage Questionnaire

Chapter 1. "I now pronounce you"

Chapter 2. "After the wedding Vows"

Chapter 3. "The Big Move"

Chapter 4. "No Mending this Marriage"

Chapter 5. "Life in Danger"

Chapter 6. " Division Brings about Divorce"

Chapter 7. "Forgiving......."Self"

Chapter 8. "Spiritually Under Construction"

Chapter 9. "Re-Acceptance"

Chapter 10. "Final Destination"

End Reflections

Dedication

First and far most I dedicate this book to God for sparing my life that I may give birth to each chapter within this book. I've dedicated these spoken words throughout this book to all individuals, family and friends who did not turn their backs on me during this fragile stage of my life. I also dedicate this book to those whom have endured trying to find themselves once again after a failed marriage.

Special Thanks...

I would like to extend a special thanks to my Bishop Arthur Ramsey, my Pastor Andrea Ramsey and my entire church family as a whole. From the bottom of my heart I release a special thanks you all. Once being reconnected to my church family, healing started to make sense to me. I thank you all for being that extended family that wanted the best for me. Thank you all for wrapping my children and I in your arms and giving us a place to call home. I thank you all for showing me that it is ok to get back up again. I can not say thank you enough...

To my spiritual Parents & church family

I've always been the type of person to give respect where respect is due. In a way I can not seem to form the correct words together to tell you all how much I love and appreciate each and every one of you. Sometimes we find ourselves going through life failing that realize that God places people in our lives for a reason. At times we may not understand that reason and it might not be for us to understand at the time. But Gods reasonings are always what matters the most.

To begin, I would like to start with My Pastor, My Spiritual Mother Andrea Ramsey! As tears begin to fall down my face as I type these words, only God knows how much I thank you for the love and care you've shared toward me. I thank you for the times you've had to discipline me. I thank you for the times you've had to get me in check. I thank you for not giving up on me when I became lost. I thank you for not turning your back on my when I turned my back on myself. I thank you for teaching me how to respect myself more as a woman. I thank you for teaching me the importance of waiting on God. I thank you for reminding me that no matter what has taken place in my life rather I caused it upon myself or rather it just happened that I am yet a child of God.

To My Bishop, my spiritual father, Arthur Ramsey! I thank you for helping me to believe in myself as a women and just because I've chosen to marry the wrong man God still has someone out her for me. I thank you for teaching me the true aspects of " no condemnation". I thank you for teaching me the importance of forgiveness and not staying parked in certain areas of your life. I thank you for reminding me that no matter what has taken place, God still loves me.

To my church family as whole I thank you all for loving on me when I returned home and helping me get back on my feet again. I thank you all for accepting my children and I into not only your lives but your hearts. My babies love each and everyone one of you all. I thank the Intercessory Prayer team for praying for me when I couldn't pray for myself! You never know the impact you have on someone's life. I can recall the day I was wanting to end my own life and I remember saying to myself sitting in that hospital, I had to make it to see my church family & spiritual parents. I thank you all for being apart of my healing process and helping me to get where God wants me to be.

With much love and respect,
Lorinda Macon

Foreword

I dare not be ashamed to tell my testimony. God has spared my life that I may give birth to every word that lies within these pages. I speak truth for healing. I release for spiritual direction! I open myself spiritually for deliverance to take place. I've organized these words within this book to extend the importance of not making moves without God. Making decisions without God will cause heartache. Over all please know that God is a forgiving God. His grace and Mercy covers you when you're unexpectedly taken out of his territory!

"A marriage without God will cause emptiness!
A marriage without God has no foundation. Without a foundation how can two build together mentally, physically and most of all spiritually?"

Two spirits mending together without the same mindset spiritually is considered as Unequally Yoked!

UnEqually Yoked

The ring was placed upon my finger and this is where it start.

He told me that he truly loved me but was it from the heart?

We went amongst family and friends and gave this marriage a seal.

As I stood before the alter everything became so real.

Every since this marriage took place, all I felt was pain.

I met him at the alter and my life was never the same.

He held my hands so tight I wanted to believe his words were true.

Was it too late for me to go backwards? Ive already said I do.

My life was taken as a joke,

This marriage should have never happened due to us both being unequally yoked…

A formed covenant

"Within a marriage a union is formed. It is no longer about one individual. The two becomes one. You believe as one, you pray as one, you seek God as one, you build as one. You hold one another up when your falling. You wipe one another's tears when your crying. In marriage you build on misunderstandings while bonding together to understand one another. You pray for one another, while standing in the gap for one another. This union should become solid with God being the head. Having no choice but to fight mentally and physically for one another against the enemy when he attempts to attack your marriage. With God you are formed into this covenant that is formed only by Him".

Introduction

After what I've experienced within the passed failures of my life, I've learned that marriage is not only hard work but it is a commitment. Most of all it is said to be a Holy Covenant formed by God.

How do you know if you are ready for marriage?
In the beginning stages of this phase in my life assuming that I was ready to be married I assumed that God sent this man into my life.
Through-out this process it became very true to me that God would never send anything into your path to distract you when your life is already under construction.

I was not able to see at the time that God was still working on me. How can I give myself to someone else if God was yet working on me? I was not ready for marriage because I did not know who I was mentally. I was not ready for marriage because I didn't know how to love me. I was not ready for marriage because I did not know how to take care of myself. I assumed that with getting married it would begin to cover up all of the empty aspects within my life.

"God honors marriage".

But what types of marriages does God truly honor?

You will know when a marriage is ordained by God. No I am not saying that marriages are perfect. Yet we are human and we are living this earthly life, but I will say that certain things should not take place in a marriage!

My marriage was not brought together by God. When I became married I lost my voice to speak the truth within that moment. I became blind of the feelings and attention given due to me being the bride. I had given up all control of my life. I merged my life with someone that had already merged his life with someone else. There was so much confusion, frustration, hurt, and betrayal! None of that is of God. I've chosen to write this book to not only share my story but to also inform how important it is to not move before God. Moving and making plans without God will end in a disaster.

It took me a while to complete this book because I became embarrassed of what truly took place in my marriage! I then quickly realized that God is a God that delivers much grace and mercy, and with much grace and mercy God spared my life to be able to give birth to each word forming the pages within this book.

Before diving into my marriage story, feel free to take advantage of this short marriage questionnaire.

Here I have a series of short questions to think about before deciding to become married...

1. Is your life set up to be in a committed marriage? If so, what steps did you take to get ready to be married?

___
___
___
___
___

2. Do you truly feel that you know your spouse?

___
___
___
___

3. Have you gone through pre-martial counseling with your Pastors?

___
___
___
___
___

4. How are finically set up for marriage?

___
___

5. What do you bring to the table for this marriage?

6. Are you equally yoked to bind your lives together spiritually?

7. What is an God ordained marriage?

8. What are your lifetime goals within being married?

9. Do you see yourself with this person for the rest of your life?

_____
_____
_____
_____
_____

10. What does an equally yoked marriage mean to you?

_____
_____
_____
_____
_____

Chapter 1
I now pronounce You...

I've never taken the time to think about what would take place after removing that beautiful floral white dress that had been shaped to my body. I've never taken time to think about what would take place after the words "I do" made an escaped from my vocal cords. I could not seem to look beyond the beautiful colors and lights that surrounded the reception hall at the "Four Points" hotel where the wedding took place. I could not seem to look beyond the ring that had been placed upon my finger connected to my left hand.

Had I just been blinded by what was truly taking place???

Did I just say "I do" to a man that deep down in my heart I knew nothing about???

What was I thinking???

Lets take a step back…

What is marriage?

Marriage is said to be a commitment which is placed between a man and a woman that loves one another. A union is formed and two individuals becomes one. Every level on each of these two individual lives are intwined and combined as one. When getting married it is very important that both individuals are on the same page or better yet the both of them together are equally yoked. The vows that are spoken amongst one another are spoken words that should hold a special bond which could not be easily broken. As I stood at the alter on July 18, 2015 my heart took a steady pace and my stomach took several dips as though I was on a rollercoaster. As my wedding vows begun to flow beneath my lips I completed the last sentence of my vows and my spirit took a leap, but sadly it was not a leap for joy.

The palm of my hands collected sweat as I begun to imagine myself throwing up all across altar floor.
Will he truly love me as he speedily spoke?
As his wife, will he truly protect me as a man should?

What I feared the most were the answers to these two questions because I did not know them for myself. I was not sure what he would do, but it surly sound good as those words took place in his vows coming through the teeth in his mouth. His eyes became glued to my eyes. As my pupils became flooded with tears he whispered to me gently "don't cry baby" "your gonna make me cry"…
What did my tears truly stand for?
Did it hit my spirit that I'd just made the biggest mistake of my life???
Was I too embarrassed to say that we needed more time to be sure we were ready to be married?

As each tear dropped from my eyes and took a position on my wedding gown, every thought and question seemed to have vanished. The excitement of becoming ones wife had taken place.
But…….
What was I truly excited for??????

The true reality of this wedding had begun to overwhelm me. There was no turning back. Too much money had been spent, too many people came to be apart. I mended my life with this man mentally, physically, spiritually and gave him the keys to my body sexually. I allowed my spirit to be intwined with an unknown spirit. When two spirits are mended together that are not equally yoked are bound to break one another down spiritually. That is the number one sign that shows that this marriage was not God ordained.

I had given this man my vow to love him and live a life with him until death do us part. Beneath the pretty white floral dress, beautiful pinned up hair, and dazzling dangling earrings deep down in my spirit I was truly afraid. I had just entered my life into a marriage convent with my eyes closed. I was not truly ready to be someones wife. But here is the thing… I went upon my own understand…

According to the "Holy Bible"
In the book of Proverbs 3:5 it states… Trust in the Lord with all your heart and lean not on your own understanding.
Living a life not led by God and leaning on your own understanding things will fall apart in the long run. They may feel good and sound good at the present moment but in the end God will reveal "Himself" through the Holy Spirit declaring you to follow the "Holy Spirit". Through many life experiences I've learned that certain things in life we bring upon ourselves when we make decisions without God. When we move without God we get lost. When plans are made without God they fall apart. When relationships are built without God there is no foundation. So I say all of this to say… When marriages are brought together without God there is no convent.

"How it began deeply for me"

I lost sight of what my goals were in life all because this man showed me a little attention. Growing up I wasn't the cutest nor the most liked or should I say not really attractive. I always attempted to wear my hair in one of those slicked down fan topped pony tails trying to resemble the look of the so called cute girls in school. I did not have the best looking clothes nor shoes. I remember getting my first job and buying my first pair of "rebox" tennis shoes. I literally wore those shoes until they only stated "box" on the side because the "re" faded away. I was a typical black girl wanting to be like the pretty girls in school. I aways assumed to myself, what man/boy would want to be with me?

I would see girls at school walking, talking and texting with their boyfriends and my self-esteem will begin to fade away. I can remember band practice one particular day and I happened to run into this guy that I had a crush on since 11th grade. It was just my luck that I left my band practice clothes in my locker. I remember running to my locker that evening at school and I happened to run right into this guy. I was flattered that not only he took time to look at me but he touched my hand.

"Yeah thats a little corny right?"

He looked at me and I looked down avoiding eye contact as I tried to control the butterflies that were swimming in my stomach. My words became frozen to him, but he seemed to have known the right words to say to me in order for me to have had sexual encounters with him weeks later. After the sex took place I never heard from him again. This had begun to confirm that something was truly wrong with me. At that moment it dawned on me that from a young age I never felt loved nor accepted. All I wanted was for someone to love me and accept me for me.

Even after I allowed a man to not only enter into my body but I allowed him to make a deposit into my spirit. It therefore made things worst for me as I thought. After many attempts of failed encounters of love I had given up. As my age expended I was bound to make the mistakes that I had made in my life. Needless to say, marriage should had been the last thing on my mind.

When you think about marriage you think about a form fitted family in a nice house surrounded by a picket white fence and a big yard for your children to play freely. It is much easier to envision things as you would like for them to be. Being married happens to be one of those things. After the so called proposal I can remember the day I went in search for the perfect wedding dress. Please allow me to say that finding the perfect wedding dress was one of the most stressful things I had ever purposely taken myself through. Getting married should have been one of the most joyous days of my life.

I guess I can say that I was happy, but was I only happy for the feelings that my body had taken hold to at that moment? Was it really the glimmer and glam that caught my eyes, and all the wedding attention given at the time. When you engage on a life journey with someone, you would think that it is very important to get to know that person before this engagement begins. Sadly this is the step I happened to miss.

Despite the confused marital mind I carried, I envisioned myself getting up in the mornings having breakfast ready for my husband. Having his work clothes ironed and shoes sitting at the front door. To make me sound much more unprepared, I even called myself purchasing two books from amazon on how to be a good wife. Now that was a bit sad if I don't say so myself. Why did I assume that a book was able to teach me to be a wife? I do not think I made it to page five in either book. After my marriage took place my husband relocated me to the state of Mississippi. In my mind I imagined arriving to Mississippi having our own home, our own car, building a family and building a foundation with one another. Spoiler alert!!!! None of that happened. We never got our own home, we never got a car together, we were hardly ever together but the only thing we shared was a bank account. These should have been red flags right away for me. Yet I allowed myself to stay because at the altar I stated until death do us part. How was I to be a good wife to him if he did not allow me to do so?

How was I to prove to him that I loved him if he did not allow me to do so. How was I to get to know who he truly was if he did not allow me to so. I had just placed my life in the hands of a man that I found myself begging to spend time with. I had just given my heart to a man that had already given his heart to someone else. Several days after the wedding my spirit had began to feel drained. Of course I had a smile on my face and seemed happy but deep down in the inside I knew that this marriage was not ordained by God.

"What does the Bible say about marriage?"

One of the main scriptures that stands out to me about marriage in the Bible is located in the book of Ephesians 5:25... According to the Holy Bible it states... "Husbands, this means love your wives, just as Christ loved the church. He gave up his life for her." I must say that I never felt as if my husband made me first. I never felt that my husband loved me. He spoke it but I never felt it. He would text it but I never felt it. In my opinion he would do things and acts as if he loved certain people on his job more than he loved me. The attention he gave me was little to nothing. It truly dawned on me that this marriage was a waste of my time.

How did I become blind at the fact that I was not truly ready to be married??? Everything happened so fast, it went from getting a ring on my finger, getting my dress made, and it seemed as if I went to bed and woke up the next day walking down to the altar. What happened to the time??? I can remember when the pastor asked if there was anyone that find a reason that these two shall not marry. As I stood there with my eyes closed I could feel my heart beat through my soul. Thinking to myself I'm sure there will be someone to rise and object to this wedding. With my eyes still closed it seemed as if time stood still. The moment I opened my eyes he yet stood before me and the wedding was yet taking place. As my eyes opened the Pastor had already stated "I now pronounce you" husband and wife. As I continued to stand before this man at the altar I thought to myself... "Now What"???

I now pronounce you "Mr. & Mrs. Macon"

In this photo I seemed to be so happy. Of course I was happy. I wanted the best out of this marriage but I could not physically do it alone. This man that I had just presented my life to had the responsibility of helping me establish the best life for us. I did not want to continue carrying the fact that I had made the biggest mistake of

my life. There was no turning back. In my mindset this was my new life now and I had to make the best of it. This was the first photo that my husband and I had taken together after the wedding. My mind had already begun to block the process of everything that had taken place not even an hour before this photo. This photo was suppose to have been the beginning of great things for the both of us to come. This photo was suppose to have symbolize the union that he and I stepped into at the altar. This photo was suppose to have symbolize the beginning of a future that we were to build together. I could not see anything else beyond this photo. I did not see the lies beyond this photo. I did not see the second life he carried beyond this photo. I did not see the love he carried for someone else beyond this photo. I did not see the confusion and hurt that was going to take place beyond this photo. I did not see me wanting to end my own life looking beyond this photo. I did not see myself yet searching for love beyond this photo. I did not see myself yet searching for attention beyond this photo. I did not see myself living alone beyond this photo. I did not see myself fighting alone beyond this photo. All I wanted was to be loved. I wanted to be held and cherished. I wanted to be respected and acknowledged. I gave up everything just to lose everything. But in the mist of losing everything God was restoring my life back together. God was already mending my heart so that I may love again. God was already mending my life so that I may live again. God was already paving the way so that I may be able to mentally walk again. God was already collecting the broken pieces of my life so that he can put me back together again. I had to find my way back to God so that I may be able to see that God yet loved me even after giving up everything including my trust in God to follow the dreams and hopes of a man. I didn't need a man to tell me that I was beautiful. I didn't need a man to live a prosperous life. I didn't need a man to make me feel more than a woman. So where did I go wrong? How did I get to this stage of my life where I assumed I needed a man for these things?

The First Dance

This photo took me to a place where all I could do was cry. I can only think about this day as he wrapped his arms around me and promised to cherish me and take care of me. I never wanted the moment in this photo to end, but sadly he brought it to an end on his terms when he decided to love someone else other than me. For a while all I could think was what was it about me? Was I not cute enough? Was I not skinny enough, was I not brown enough? What was it? Why didn't I see the signs before my feelings became deeply involved. Why did I become so consumed in the life this man said he would provide for me? Even after being confronted of who he truly was, why did I still want to be with him? I truly believed that I loved him as a person, and as for who he was. But why couldn't he be truthful with me? This moment took me to a place where I assumed God sent this man into my life. But when you become so blind to the true aspects that are taking place you begin to accept anything that is presented into your life. Especially if you already feel as if know one else would want you, you're quick to accept the first things that are thrown into your direction. As I think about unforeseen situations that had already taken place

in my life all I wanted was to be loved. I wanted to belong to someone. I wanted to truly know how it felt to be married. I wanted a man to tell me that I was beautiful. I wanted to enjoy sex the way a woman deserved to enjoy sex. After years of dealing with being raped, I wanted to know how it felt to freely have sex and not have to question myself. I wanted that intimacy part of my life back. I wanted the sexuality part of my life back. I wanted the control of my life back. Needless to say, none of these things were accomplished within this marriage. This is what happens when moving and making decisions without God. Things become harder to withhold.

Chapter 2
After the Wedding Vows

The two doors began to open I can hear the song I had chosen to walk down to the altar to begin to play, which was "Giving Myself" by Jennifer Hudson. The doors opened to the conference room and my heart began to pound when everyone began to rise giving respects to the bride as she made her entrance. All I could think about was I still had the opportunity to put an end to all of this. I still had the opportunity to put a hold to a mistake that was going to change my life forever. As the lyrics of the song continued to play it dawned on me that this was really happening.

I am giving myself to a man that I hardly knew anything about. To be clearly honest to this day I can't even say I know his birthday by heart. I can remember being on the phone with him nearly a month or so before the wedding and we went back and forth asking one another questions about one another as though we were studying for a major exam. This was only another red flag as to why this wedding should not have never taken place.

In life God presents to us so many red flags when we are heading in the wrong direction. When we are distracted by what is in the mist of our eye sight all red flags are missed. When we ignore red flags we cause problems in the future to take place. After I directly ignored all the red flags that were presented in this situation I had to face reality! I had just gotten married and yet the both of us together were unequally yoked! In a way I did not feel any different. After the day came to an end and we made it to our hotel room I said quietly to myself, "I've spoken the vows I've studied and memorized over the passed two weeks, what do we do now???

"Where the hurt starts for me..."

The wedding was finally over! The reception was finally over! It was time for the two of us to spend some quality time with one another. We arrived to the hotel room, the room was beautifully decorated with a flower pedal pathway walking in the entrance. The bathtub was filled with bubbles and red flower pedals. I thought to myself, "Oh my goodness" we were about to have an amazing night. We sat in the bed and and opened all of our wedding gifts and cards receiving over thousands of dollars in money. We were delighted to say that the money would help us get a good start in where we were planning to move in days to come. After opening all gifts and cards, the both of us got into the bath tub filled with bubbles and flower pedals. For some odd reason he left his boxers on as though it was a swimming pool. I was a bit confused. "*I guess I missed something*".

    I proceeded to get into the bathtub the way I wanted to. I assumed this was to be something romantic! I was completely wrong. It was far from romantic. I thought to myself is this how I should feel right after getting married? After sitting in the tub "*playing with bubbles*" I'll say, we both got out, and got dressed for bed. The hotel presented us with two white robs and white slippers. Lying together in bed time continued to pass, I was not ready for the day to end. The feelings that were cringed in my heart had begun to over flow. It truly hit me the I had just gotten married. But, here is the scary part, I was afraid of what was going to take place for us. I knew I had just given up everything for this man. My home, my job, my family and my church family. I turned my back on everything. I had nothing to turn back to. "What was I thinking?
That's the problem, "***I wasn't thinking***".

So the wedding part was over, and there I was in the hands of a man that I assumed I knew everything about. I only went on his words. "I TRUSTED HIM", I believed in him, I spoke up for him, I walked behind him, I belittled myself for him, I gave up my life for him. This is what I settled for! Back to the wedding night... The both of us got into bed, it was such a big relief to get the wedding over with. I was ready for a relaxing night. I was ready to enjoy this night with my husband. I lied there thinking to myself, "sure enough he's going to grab me and hold me or something"!!! I WAS WORNG ONCE AGAIN... I peeked over at him and there he was on his phone. " ***Well I'll be damn***" Is he really on his phone? This can't be real! I turned around and attempted to get comfortable.

    I've waited so long for this special moment. Who wouldn't want to have an amazing night of romantic sex after getting married? "Was I expecting too much?" We lied there for hours and this man did not lay a finger on me. I attempted to move my body closer to him thinking that he would get the signal, and still nothing! I was confused once again! "Was I suppose to ask for sex after the wedding"? I thought again to myself, I guess I'm suppose to ask! I turned to him and asked, are we going to have sex? He responded "Not tonight, he's tired"! I turned back over and moved back closer to my side. At this point we're lying back to back to one another.

    He was so tired but there he was on his phone having a great conversation through a game app with a man, at that moment I became more disappointed in myself. I began to have that feeling I had in high school when I felt as if no one wanted me. This time it was a bit different. I've just given my life to this man, so why weren't we having sex on our wedding night? What was happening in his phone that was so important? It was truly becoming real that I had made the biggest mistake of my life! Will it be this way for the rest of our marriage, is all I could ask myself! I wasn't sure. I've never been married before. Don't get me wrong, it was not all about sex. It was about the moment and his actions. So of course I wanted sex, but it did not happen that night. Something in his phone took hold to his attention before I did. As I continued to lie there tears had begun to fall from my eyes. I should've not been feeling this way if I was happily married. I should've not been feeling that way if this marriage was ordained by God. I would have not been feeling that way if I would have listened to God when he said "your not ready daughter!" Why didn't I listen??? Nothing is more clearer than the voice of God when you are connected with God and intwined with the plan God has for your life. I went through life creating different avenues for my life because I was lost. When this took place, the plans God had for my life had be interrupted.

    I begun to feel separated from everything in my life. When things that are connected to your life aren't of God, we give room for destruction in our lives. So needless to say, the destruction had begun! While in the mist of destruction it was easy to allow the enemy to come in and take control. Some way, somehow you begin to long for a way out. You seek for help, but.... was it too late for me???

Chapter 3
The Big Move

After getting married we'd talked about moving me to the state of Mississippi. I did not think he would move me that soon, meaning I was going to have to leave my job that I've been at for over 8 years at the time. My home and my church home. Without thinking too much about it, I decided to take the move. Directly after the wedding we moved to Mississippi. It was about 3 days after the wedding to be exact. I had begun to get excited! I assumed it would be a great beginning. Having our own home, new job, new people, new surroundings, on top of being newly weds. In the process of preparing to make this big move to Mississippi I had begun to feel completely out of order.

Despite of my feelings I acted as if everything was ok, and I did all that I was able to do in my being to make the best of the situation. I felt as if nothing was right, almost like I was not complete. My body took hold to this uncomfortable feeling that I could not seem to get rid of. Things were changing in my life and these changes were taking place way too fast. The changes happened so fast my spirit wasn't able to keep up. My spirit was beginning to feel drained. I was no longer myself. Even after being married, I smiled and seemed happy but in the inside, my spirit was broken!

"What was beginning to happen to me???"

With getting married and moving to Mississippi I had begun to just go with the flow. Whatever my husband wanted me to do I did it. Where ever he wanted me to go I went. Where ever he did not want me to go I did not go. There was no sense of direction within me. There was no sense of peace within me. Before this move to Mississippi took place, my husband discussed with me about living with his mother for a couple of weeks when we arrived to Mississippi until we were able to get our own place. Needless to say, we were there way beyond the couple of weeks originally discussed. Days, weeks and months had passed and we were yet living in his bedroom at his mothers home.

Don't get me wrong, I did appreciate his mom from the bottom of my heart for opening her doors to her son and I. But there comes a point to where we needed our own. There were several things I was not allowed to do because we were living with his mother. Let's not forget that there as little to no sexual activity. It had gotten to a point to where I was begging for sex. He finally told me that he did not feel comfortable having sex in his mother's home. I've even brought up the idea of getting an hotel room several times. He always told me that when we got into our own home things will begin to fall in place for us. Again, that never happened! There was no personal time between him and I. There was no him and I outings, there was no "US!"

My husband had many females friends in Mississippi. I'll say because of his personality he carried. He was very opened minded and out going, not like any typical man I'll say. Every chance he had he was out with his female friends so he says. Ok, so let's set something straight, this is not in any way to bash him or talk badly about him! This was truly our lives, our marriage and things that truly took place! He was who he was, and I accepted that because I was so blinded of the fact that I actually married him.

My heart couldn't handle the fact that after we'd gotten married there was no honeymoon. I was a women that was easily pleased so I didn't care if we went on a two day honeymoon or just an over night honeymoon somewhere away. Instead, he took me to Dave & Bustards. If your not familiar what Dave & Busters is, its basically a Chuck E Cheese for adults. I tried my best to enjoy my night and be appreciative. I did not want to create an argument on the day we were married. I'd open heartily decided to just go with the flow. I became very content with things that had begun to take place in our marriage. I kept my mouth closed and I accepted any and everything because I didn't want to be rejected. If he said go I went. If he said stay, I stayed. If he said don't call just text, then texting it was. I took notice that my husband has begun to minimize me from his life. He only brought me up when it was convent for him. Yet this is what I accepted, this is what I married into, this is what I chose to live with because I was afraid to ask for help or afraid to say that I made the biggest mistake of my life. This is who I chose to share a life with because I thought he was my other half. This is who I chose to share a bed with. This is the life I settled for because I thought it was too late that I'd already said "I do". This was all new to me so of course all I did was agreed to things that were confronted to me. I felt like I agreed on all the things that mattered the most within our marriage, but somehow it still wasn't enough. I allowed him to get away with anything because I was afraid I was going to lose him. There were nights where he got up and got dressed claiming that he was taking a midnight run. & of course in the beginning I was dumb enough to believe him. Some nights coming back inside smelling like Gods knows what! Yet he jumps in the shower and right into bed as if nothing happened. I kept my mouth closed, I didn't even have the strength to bring myself to question him of his destinations during the middle of the night. The truth made itself known at the right time. Even though I remained silent, God heard my cry through my silence.

  I silently begun to lose respect for my husband. If he couldn't be honest with me about the smallest things, being honest with the bigger things were definitely a task for him. This is where I became mute. Becoming mute kept the status of our arguments on an all time low. Now that I've found myself out of this marriage I've learned that being mute only allowed him to continue to do what he was doing with no questions ask and no consequences. Being mute gave him complete control over this marriage than what he already had & this is where I went completely wrong. This only made me weaker. It became easier for him to walk over me. It became easier for him to talk over me. It became easier for him to not want to touch me or have sex with me. It became easier for him to make decisions and plans without me. I basically became absolutely to him. God begun to show me certain things that I had no choice but to accept. Months within our marriage, there was no sex. "NONE" what so ever. No four play, no touching, nothing! I couldn't seem to understand why. There were several nights where there was only him and I home alone and he yet chose not to touch me. I did not want my first thought to be, "if he wasn't getting it from me then he was surly getting it from somewhere else". As a women, how can you not think that? Before the truth made an escape from his mouth, I already knew what the business was....

When becoming mute in a marriage things like this begins to happen. My husband picked me up from work one morning, and we made a stop to a local gas station before going home. He proceeded to get out of the car to go pay for & pump gas. As he sat down getting back into the car, I couldn't help but to see a bandage slapped across the lower part of his hip. At this moment I knew that being silent wasn't going to fix this situation. When arriving home I simply asked " Whats the bandage for on his hip." He contained to do what he was doing as though I had not said a word. So I asked again, threatening to leave him. In my heart I knew I wasn't leaving. Like seriously where was I going to go??? But I had to find some strength somewhere that he might begin to take me somewhat serious. It wasn't until nearly a week later he came out and told me that he had contracted a STD, and this is why he wasn't having sex with me. At that moment I died inside. How could this be possible. How could he have contracted a STD if him and I had not had sex in months. I remember puling myself together asking him how & why.

All he did was cried saying that he promised he was not going to have sex with him again...

WAIT.... WAIT....WAIT... YES YOU HEARD ME RIGHT "HIM"...

This man held my hand at the altar and promised to love me, respect me and honor me but how can this be if he continues to have sex with men!

What was I suppose to do?

At that moment, I needed someone to talk to. I needed someone to wrap their arms around me and tell me that things would be ok. I needed someone to tell me that this was all a dream. Days had passed and I was yet with my husband. I did not know what to do. In our vows stated til death do us part. Neither one of us had died, but I can say that I was spiritually beginning to die in the inside.

"...This is where it became real..."

Shortly after moving to Mississippi, my husband planned a trip to Atlanta, Georgia. Now remind you, we had no extra money to spend, nothing of our own just yet. Why was this trip to Atlanta so important to him. To make this worst, he planned it for himself! I wasn't allowed to go. When I say my feelings were beyond hurt they were truly hurt. We didn't have a honeymoon but he took it upon himself to take a trip alone to Atlanta. What was happening in Atlanta to where I could not be there? What was so important in Atlanta to where he left me in Mississippi where I knew no one but his mother, so of course I was left in the house everyday by myself. I did not know who to call nor talk to because I was afraid that people would say, "I told you so!". What was I to do? Who was I to talk to? There I was married but alone. There I was married but didn't feel loved.

There I was married but wasn't connected to anything. Lying in bed alone in my husbands mom home, I picked up my phone to call my husband. I called several times and I did not get an answer. What was he doing so important to where he was not able to talk to me. We were married why was I alone. Why wasn't he answering my calls? Hours later he decided to give me a call back. I was so disappointed and sad, I no longer wanted to speak with him any longer that day. For the rest of his Atlanta trip I hardly heard anything from him. Upon his returning from Atlanta things were different. Nothing was the same. My first thought was... "What really happened in Atlanta? Things became very weird in our marriage. I felt different, in a way to where I began to lose trust in my husband. After his returning from Atlanta, I came across several pictures posted on social media of him and three other men. I knew I was not tripping but I knew for sure that two of the men posed in these photos with my husband were gay. Instantly the devil took over my thoughts. All I could think about was what business did my husband have in Atlanta with these gay men? Days had passed and I must say that time had healed that moment because I forgave him and let it go. Why was I so stupid??? That was clearly another red flag from God, but here again I ignored it. Days passed and things had seemed to get worse. I was beginning to pick up certain vibes from my husband. I began to notice that every time I would take a shower and come into our bedroom and get dressed he would leave the room. Every time I would come into the room and change clothes he would leave the room. I then finally realized that my husband did not like to see me naked. He was not attracted to me. Yet this was the man that I had married. This was the man that I had just given my life to. This was the man that I had just gave up my life for. This was yet something else that I allowed to float right through me.

    I was finally able to land a job in Mississippi. I was hired in as a supervisor in the EVS department on the Island View Casino Resort. It was an amazing job, but there was one down fall. This was the same location my husband had been employed. He had been working at the Island View for nearly two years, and once I was hired I found that he was well known throughout all departments of the casino. Once being hired no one knew me, but they did know of me as being Mr. Macon's wife. Quickly news got around that I was married to him and I had been hired in as a supervisor. After being there for some time I began to get close to many supervisors working along with me. Sooner than later there were a number of individuals coming to me informing me that they knew my husband and that he was 100% gay. At this moment I was not accepting it. I could not accept it. I was married to this man, how was I to accept this? Why did I truly believe he was changed or he could have changed.

    It took one specific lady to pull me to the side and speak with me. I could tell that she had taken some time to pull together all of her evidence before talking with me. I remember clearly the evening we sat in the EDR, which was the cafeteria where the employees ate lunch. This lady began to show me pictures of my husband dressed up as a woman. Wearing heels, dresses, lipstick and some pictures he had on makeup. I got so sick to my stomach, I could not speak, I could not move, I could not think. But the scary thing was, why was I still in denial? I had just married this man and he was completely gay. What did I miss? How could I have missed this?

After seeing these pictures, days and weeks had passed I decided not to say anything to him. We hardly saw one another because I was working the grave yard shift at the job. Finally it hit me once again that I'd made the biggest mistake of my life. But… was I stuck? Was my life ruined? I had begun to feel completely uncomfortable around my own husband. Just when I thought things couldn't get any worse, the devil showed himself again. On this particular day my husband sat his phone on the charging dock in the bedroom while he went to shower. He was one that always had his phone locked. I've never seen a phone so loaded with passcodes. It became very shocking to me that his phone was unlocked as music was played from it while sitting on the charging dock. His phone made a dinging noise as though he had a text message from someone. I leaned over to take a look and noticed that it was not a text message but it was a "game message alert". When the phone made an alert it happened to stop the music so I proceeded to pick up his phone to close the notification from the game to allow the music to continue playing. When clicking to game notification it opened. I then noticed that it was a message from a male through the game messenger. My husband was a very sneaky individual. Who would ever think about messaging someone through a game message? "He surly did"!

I proceeded to open the game messenger and to my findings I see that my husband and this male had been conversing back and forth for months. I skimmed through the messages and the more I read the more my stomach began to lose control of itself. The message that hit me the hardest was when this man asked my husband how his anal felt, and that he should bring more vaseline next time. The conversations between this man and my husband were beyond disappointing and disgusting.. From that day forward it was conformation that my husband was truly "yet" a gay man. I placed his phone back on the charging dock and lied in bed. Tears began to uncontrollably roll down my face. My body froze. It seemed as if I couldn't breath. As I laid there, my life flashed before my eyes. It became more clear to me as to why this man did not want to touch me, cuddle with me or even have sex with me. Even after knowing that this was truly my husbands lifestyle, I yet waned him to tell me what I could possibly do to help him change. Not accepting the fact that there was nothing I could physically do to change this man that I had married.

He was not physically attracted to me. I questioned myself over and over again, why did I truly believe he was straight? Why did I put myself in this situation? As days passed everything was making more sense to me. My husband was guy, but I needed to find out why this man married me??? In a why I blamed myself for allowing things to get as far as they had gotten. There was plenty of opportunity to turn back, but I allowed my emotions and feelings to take hold of me. What do I do now???

I was all the way in Mississippi, where was I to go? I knew hardly anyone to just get up and leave, I didn't know the area nor was I familiar with the city of Gulfport. Because I was so afraid to leave after everything that had taken place, I stayed. I stayed in the marriage, I stayed in his mother's home, I stayed in Mississippi. I had begun to find different things in my husbands room that had given me more conformation. Photos that would have anyone confused. Clothing that were cut up to a women's likings that he had worn. The more things I began to discover the more I felt as if the devil had grabbed my life, balled it up and threw it in the trash.

I had to find a way out! I felt stuck. I had to say something. One day when I pulled together enough strength to ask my husband what was going on. I could not seem to pull the words together of what to say. But it came close enough. The words slip out so fast, I couldn't hear them myself. I can remember asking him two questions!

The first question was... "Why did you bring me along?"

The second question was... "Did you you use condoms when being sexually active with these men?" The answers he had given me to these questions were not acceptable for me to even continue the conversation with him! I was truly heart broken. I felt disgusting. All I could think about was getting to a "Health Department" the next morning and getting tested.

After all results had returned from the STD\HIV testing, I can remember sitting at the end of his bed with all of my belongings packed. I did not have much but all I wanted was my clothing. He came home from work and saw all my things packed, I said to him I cannot do this anymore. I can not stay here! As I spoke those words I had no clue where I was going. I went to work that night with bags of clothes in my car. I sat at work and I could not seem to take hold to what had taken place. All I could think about was where I would lay my head once my work shift was over.

Before the night was over, I did begin to talk with another supervisor. I can remember telling her that I did not have a place to stay. This lady did not know me from the back of her hand. She opened her home to me. God had begun to show me that he did not give up on me. He begun to show me that there was a way out. He begun to show me that it was ok to say I made a mistake. He begun to show me that my life was not over, in fact, it was just beginning. I had to truly accept that this man and I was not equally yoked. This marriage should have never taken place.

Chapter 4
No Mending this Marriage

At this point of our marriage my husband and I were separated. I felt as if everything was my fault. I asked God to teach me to be more wise, and understanding to what was happening in front of my eyes. So many things went through my mind. I was not able to deal with the feelings that were captured within me. I began questioning myself. Did I make the right decision leaving my husband after truly acknowledging that he was a gay man?

Did I truly believe in my mind that he would change? Was this something that could truly be fixed? Why did I still believe that we could be a couple despite of this? I moved into my supervisors home that night after leaving work. Weeks had passed and I had begun to feel very uncomfortable as if I was out of place. I wanted things to be better more like how they were before this marriage. But deeply inside I knew I was not able to move back to his mothers home. Or better yet I was afraid to move back to his mothers home. After many individuals concernedly expressing to me not to marry this man I did so anyway. This dark feeling came upon me. My mind went blank as though I couldn't see myself out of any of this.

To my understanding there was only one way out. I went into this ladies bathroom and spotted a blue bottle of pills sitting on a brown shelf. Needless to say I was not aware of what the pills were for. I knew I wanted to die but I did not want to feel any pain in the process. After seeing many movies and TV shows I'd learned that by taking a lot of pills that was the easiest way to go. I sat on the floor in the bathroom and proceeded to open the bottle of pills. I poured an unknown amount of pills in the palm of my hand. I sat on the side of the toilet thinking that I would change my mind, by making myself throw up immediately after taking them. I can remember asking God to forgive me but I was tired. I can remember asking God to forgive me but there was no fixing this mistake.

I can remember asking God to forgive me but there was no other way out of this situation! Without doing too much more thinking I swallowed the pills I poured into my hand. After taking the pills I sit on the side of the toilet right next to the bathtub. Nothing instantly took place so I assumed that it did not work. I sat there sobbing because I wanted to be gone off the face of this earth. It was maybe about an hour later my head begun spinning. My stomach started to feel not so good. I tried standing up to get over the toilet because I felt like I was going to throw up. In the mist of trying to stand up, I fell to the floor.

The next thing I can possibly remember is waking up in Garden Park hospital located in Gulfport MS. Mrs Hilda, which was the supervisor I had been living with asked me why did I attempt to do such a thing? Sadly I could not seem to answer her at the time. I did not understand why I was still living, why couldn't they have just allowed my to die? With tears running down my face I asked her how did she know I had taken those pills. She said that she saw the pill bottle floating in the toilet. I couldn't even recall putting the pill bottle in the toilet. Once I was confronted with reality it instantly hit my spirit that I tried to kill myself.

"Where did I go wrong?"

Everything seemed as if it fell apart, from the first day I stepped foot at the altar, I placed my life in the hands of a man that was not interested in me. Why did it take me so long to discover this? I had given up my identity just to be with this man. I had given up who I was just to be with this man. I had given up everything. I left my life behind to be this man's life. When becoming married to someone the two of you become one, but you should never lose yourself or forget who you are. When I became married I lost connection with myself. I lost my connection with God. I lost my connection with the Holy Spirit. My life was introduced to an unknown territory! I began fighting with my own spirit! "How would I ever find myself back". I had always wondered would my life ever be the same?

Once I had been brought back to a stabled place in the hospital I assumed that I would be discharged. Guess what I was wrong once again. I was admitted to Gulf Coast Mental Health Center. I remained there under observation for three days. While there I had nothing but time to think about what had taken place. When attempting to commit suicide the true aspects of this never hit your spirit until after the fact. It hit my spirit that I gave up on myself. That fast, I had given up on God! That fast, my faith had begun to vanish. I became deaf to the voice of God. I'd became blind to the vision that God had for my life. The longer I stayed in that mental Institution it seemed as if I became more suicidal, and I was only there for three days. Until the third day I was there my spirit took hold to something. Quickly I was reminded in my spirit that Jesus rose on the third day! On the third day he got up!!! He got up so that we may live again. He got up so that we can be forgiven. He got up so that we may be able to start over again. He got up so that we a be born again!

On that third day of being in that institution, my spirit began to reconnect with God. I remember being in the room alone and I fell to my knees crying and asking God not to give up on me. It clearly hit my spirit that only God was going to pull me out of this. I heard repeatedly in my spirit that this marriage cannot be mended. The two of us were unequally yoked. I had no business with this man. It was time for me to rise up and make some major decisions. But I could not do that without God. I could not mentally take a stand without God. I'd already made so many wrong choices without God. It was time for me to allow God to have his way. I had to come at peace with it all and truly accept that this marriage should have never taken place.

Why did I continue to fight for something that God did not put together??? I began to realize that there was not anything else I could physically put forth in this marriage. It had gotten to a point to where I did not know how to forgive my husband any longer. I held so much inside to where I did not know how to release it so I assumed that shutting myself down was the fastest way out. Something had to give, and I quickly learned that my life wasn't it. It was time for me to fight for Lorinda physically, mentally and spiritually to get my life back!

Chapter 5
Life in Danger!

In my opinion one of the biggest things that feared me the most was contracting a sexually transmitted disease once realizing who my husband was and what he was doing with other men. The date everything came out I could not get to my doctors office fast enough in Gulfport, Mississippi. I can remember asking my husband if he used protection while engaging in sexual activity with these men and of course he told me yes, but I knew it was not the truth! When ever you engage in sexual activity with individuals other than your spouse, you are opening doors for danger. You are welcoming that person's sprint and sexual history not only into your life but into your spouses life as well.

The day I found out my husband was still having sex with men I truthfully envisioned myself sitting in my doctors office and as the words "Lorinda you are HIV positive" came form his lips! I envisioned that my doctor came in telling me that I had contracted a STD! Is it bad to say that I had already prepared myself mentally to expect the worst??? I was prepared to live my life accepting the fact that I'd placed my life in danger. I can remember getting a call from my doctors office on a Friday morning.

I vividly remember on a Friday because I receive the call while I was at work at the Island View Casino doing my Friday morning counts for product. I quickly recognized the number when it appeared on my phone screen. At that moment the fear that flooded heart would not allow me to answer the call. I feared what the person on the other end of the phone would say. At that moment I knew that I wasn't ready to face this reality. The ring on my phone ended and seconds later a voicemail alert popped up. For some reason it made my feelings worst. It's sad to say that it bothered my spirit even more to listen to the voicemail.

  I pulled myself together realizing that whatever it was I would have to face it regardless. I preceded to listen to the voicemail attempting to recall what the voicemail stated. After listening it stated that it was very important for me to contact the Gulfport Women's health Center on this concern at my earliest convenience. All I could think about was my life being over. In my head I had already convinced myself that I had HIV. I had already prepared myself to accept the worst news of my life. The devil had already won in my mind. He succeeded in ruining my life. That fast once again I wanted to be dead all over again. "Why did I deserve to live"...

  I felt like in my mind I was dying slowly. After all of this fighting against my mind, I yet had to return my doctors office call. I made up in my mind that I was not going to call back. I decided to go inside the location. I remember walking in and the lady at the reception desk asked if I was there for a scheduled appointment. I replied "No Ma'am I'm actually here to speck with someone, I received a phone call and a voicemail but the voicemail did not give too much information pertaining my results. With fear in my voice my eyes began to tear up. She instructed me to have a seat after asking for my name. Finally another lady came out to speak directing me in the back room with the burgundy door.

  I read the poster on the wall stating "Control your life and get tested!!!" I literally read that poster about fifty times until my eyes became glued to it. The lady came and took a seat to the right of me. What became shaky to me was what lied on the papers she held in her hands. I felt like the fate of my life lied in her hands. As she began to speak, my legs shook uncontrollably. She began speaking saying... "Mrs Macon we received your results from your testing. She continues by saying you did test "NEGATIVE" for HIV. As my heart pumped with relief she says "BUT"!!! When I heard the word BUT I felt my stomach dropped.

She then continued to speak saying "You did test POSITIVE for chlamydia and gonorrhea. I literally began throwing up right where I sat. I can remember the lady grabbing this red cloth and the garbage can to assist me. Not only was I embarrassed but I was at a loss. My first thought was, how could this be! I cried uncontrollably. As she began telling me that these two std's were curable I was yet not accepting what she had just told me. I'm not sure if I wanted to accept it. But I did not have a choice but to accept it. My mind went black, I could't explain what I saw. How could he feel ok with having sex with men and coming home crawling on top of me as if everything was ok??? **HOW DARE HE???**

Just how!!! I felt disgusted. I felt like no man would ever want me again. I felt like I was always going to be alone. This was all my fault. I put myself in danger!!! After leaving the doctors office I was not sure if I should contact my husband or not. But come to find out he was already infected and decided not to tell me. Days later he decided he was ready to tell me that he was infected. This clearly shows me that this man didn't care anything about me. I trusted him!!! I placed my life in his hands. Again I placed my life in danger. That fast, those std's could have easily been HIV or AIDs. That fast those std's could have been something that was not curable. What finally calmed my spirit was when I was told by my doctor that as long as I took the antibiotics that were provided as instructed and until they were gone things would be ok. From that day forward I was tested for HIV every three months and by the grace of God, all results came back NEGATIVE. I had to get myself back to a healthy state in life. I had to take care of me!!! There was no turning back.

Chapter 6
Division Brings about Divorce

Could it be true that I was afraid to move forward because I did not ever want to experience being alone again? The devil will have your mind believing that you belong in the situations that your life is in. He will pump things up to make them the main attractions of your life to where you can not focus on anything else but what is at hand. All I thought about was not being with my husband anymore. All I thought about was the bad decisions I had made. All I thought about was being alone again. To be truthfully honest, The subject of getting a divorce bothered me.

I wasn't strong enough to talk about it without crying. Matter of a fact, the thought of getting a divorce put so much fear In me and made me feel as if I had to accept my husband for who he was. Deeply in my heart I knew what needed to take place but without any guidance how would a divorce take place? Because it was I that wanted the divorce to happen did it mean it was all my fault??? I feared that everything will be turned right back or me. We had spent so much money, there were so many people involved, an so many feelings involved! So much in my life had changed in those couple of months. Why did I really want the divorce??? Was it that my husband did not truly love me?

What is it that he placed these men that he was sexually attracted to before me? What is it that he lied to me? What is it that his vows that he stated to me at the altar amongst family and friends were a lie? Sadly it was all of these aspects and more! Each of these aspects took a position as to why this divorce must take place. We did not have anything any longer. How can you built on a lie? When building a relationship on a lie there is no stability! With no stability things will begin to fall apart. Do I stay and continue to allow things to fall apart? Do I stay and continue to leave my life open to dangerous territory? Or do I make the first step into leaving???

At this point I do not want to see my husband neither did I want to be in the same room with him. So I must say that this is where most of the texting amongst the both of us came about. He was already big at the texting thing. He would rather text me than talk to me face to face. This specific day I knew it was time. Time was up for dragging one another along the way. Time was up for not knowing what to do. It was time that I sent the most important message of my life. For about three hours I let the four words "I want a divorce" sit in my send bar on my phone before sending it to him. Something kept me from pushing that send button.

I felt in my heart that after sending that message it will open up an entire new platform for the two of us. And just as I imagined it did!!! He responded as if I did something wrong by asking for a divorce. How could he not think that this was coming??? Did he seriously think that what he was doing was OK! Did he seriously think that I had to accept what was going on!!! Did he seriously text me back stating that we needed more marriage counseling!!! I said to myself... "What part of my text did he not understand???"...

Marriage counseling cannot change the fact that you decided to have sex with men rather than your wife! Marriage counseling will not change the fact that I had to give up my life for a lie. Marriage counseling was not going to change the fact that I had to return home and face not only my family and friends but my Pastors! Marriage counseling was not going to prepare me for all the "I told you so's" I was going to receive!!! No marriage counseling was going to prepare me for any of this... we finally set a date to meet at the courthouse to begin filing for the divorce. Upon arrival we exchanged rings with one another, returning each ring to its original owner.

Even though the divorce was not yet complete, removing that ring was a sense of relief for me. Some may say how??? I can not truly explain it, but it gave me some type of relief, almost like I didn't belong to him anymore!!! We both sat at this brown table in a room at the courthouse to begin filling out paperwork. Why did this feel so wrong??? This should not be happening!!! We should be happily married, we should be moving into our own home preparing to build a family together. But none of that was taking place. At this moment everything felt so wrong!!!

It felt wrong for me because I took my vows serious! I took our marriage serious, I fought and fought and fought into there was no more fight left in me! I accepted this and I accepted that until there was no more room to accept anything else. My heart did not beat the same anymore. My feelings cannot be explained anymore. Deep down in my heart and spirit this had to take place! The division within our lives brought about this divorce. This wasn't only about my husband and the mistakes he had made.

As I begun to truthfully think about everything, I made the biggest mistake of all!!! That mistake was not listening to the voice of God. When you fail to listen to the voice of God and it will bring about confusion, hurt and pain. One thing I know for sure is that when God is in the mist, confusion would never have a place! Another mistake I made was not loving myself enough to pull back when I had the opportunity to do so. I did not love myself to say "Lorinda this relationship is not healthy, you do not deserve this"! I did not love myself enough to seek help when help was needed. I became ashamed to ask for help and guidance because I had already thrown nearly a year of my life away. Even though those days weeks and months cannot be replaced, God can always give me a new beginning. After everything that had taken place I felt in my heart and believed that ending this marriage was best for the both of us!

Chapter 7
Forgiving "Self"

It came to a point to where I had moved on with my life. At that moment I made the decision to remain in Mississippi because I had a very good job, which paid me very well. Eventually I was on my feet and I was able to get my own place. "My God" was it the best feeling ever! I wasn't sure but I somehow felt that I made myself move on with my life. But on every level I did not move on. Deep down inside I was still hurting. So of course I found ways to cover up that hurt. Instead of trying to truly heal I found things to overlay the heart. I can say that I carry so much hurt within me that I have began to give up on love. But honestly I wasn't giving myself enough time.

This is where this situation came about. When you open doors in your life while not giving time for other doors to close, you are giving room for the enemy to come in and have his way. Needless to say I didn't give myself time to heal I just kept going! After I had moved away from the failure of my marriage, and remaining in Mississippi I met this guy at my job. I knew from day one that I did not have any business with this man. But my mind was on another mission, I wanted to be loved, I wanted to be cared for. I wanted to recover from all the dumb mistakes that I had made. This man showed interest in me and I couldn't pass that up. I had given his man my phone number and I can remember the first night he took me out.

He took me to dinner at the "Beau Rivage Casino"! He even got two nights at the hotel attached to the casino. I then remember engaging in sexual activity with this man. All I could think about was the previous months that lead my life into this broken puzzle. Why did I think that this night of sex with this man would take my mind off of everything? For the moment it worked! It had been months before any man laid hands on me. Or shall I say it had been months since my husband had laid hands on me. I couldn't remember what it felt like to be held by a man. I couldn't remember what it felt like to be cuddled up with a man. I must say that this was an amazing night. At the moment I felt like him and I were going to do an idol!

Was I Trippin!

Yeah I think I was Trippin! After the two nights we spent at the hotel, he dropped me off at home. Days later I then noticed that communication between him and I drop down to slim to nothing. It went from getting a good morning text every morning to once a week to nothing at all. I will call him and he wouldn't return my call until weeks later. I had decided that I had to find a way to get over him, I then truly realized that it was definitely something I did to get my mind off my failed marriage and divorce. It was just another stupid mistake that I had made! I remember being at work weeks later and I had fallen very sick. I couldn't understand why I was so sick. It then came to me that I had not received my cycle. I knew then that something was really wrong. I got off work that morning and went to Walmart to get a pregnancy test. For some reason I wasn't nervous at all.

Reading the instructions on the test it stated to wait three minutes before reading the results. After taking a test two lines began to deeply fade into this pink color way before the three minutes had passed. This was true I was surely pregnant. I knew that I had to get in contact with this man. I was finally able to reach him and tell him about the pregnancy. I knew in my heart that this should not be happening I should not be pregnant! My marriage has fallen apart and now I am pregnant by another man that I knew nothing about. I had to ask myself, am I mentally, physically and spiritually ready to raise a baby? How can I love this child when I didn't love myself? I needed God like never before!!! I decided to tell this man that I wanted to move back home to Illinois.

I asked him if he would like to move back with me. Maybe this was my chance that I could really form a family! At that moment he hit me with the hardest news ever! He told me that he was a registered sex offender and that he would have a difficult time attempting to leave the state of Mississippi, and also stating that his life was not sat up for a child as though my life was. At that moment I knew that something was seriously wrong with me!!!
What do I do to attract these type of men??? I knew that I had to make moves without him pregnant in all. I finally moved back to Illinois it was like starting all over again. There I was, back in Illinois I had to find a way to rebuild again. I had to find a way to mend my body from what I had accepted.
But how was I going to do this???

To begin, I had to truly know what it meant to forgive myself. I had to learn and understand that forgiving myself was an essential step that had to take place in the healing process of my life. By not forgiving myself I was unknowingly placing myself into this box of where I was in complete remembrance of everything that had taken place. My heart and my mental state had to be inline with one another.

Having to realize that it was ok to move on. Reminding myself that was ok to start over again. It was ok to say that I screwed up. It was ok to say that I was at a dead end and had nowhere else to turn. Forgiving myself gave me the keys to the doors that stood before me entering into the next stages of my life. Forgiving myself gave me the ability to take responsibility of the direction in which my life was going from here. Forgiving myself did not mean that I had to forget what happened. By forgiving myself I was now able to use my experiences as testimonies one in which is writing this book. Most importantly it was a must that I begun to forgive myself so that true healing was able to take place. It came to a point to where forgiveness was detrimental because the hurt and pain of the entire situation was beginning to consume me. I was allowing this situation to control my life. This was again another area of my life where I gave up control. There where moments where I thought I forgave myself but I quickly realized that I was yet holding onto the emotions of this part of my life. I was holding on to the mishaps that took place of this part of my life. I was holding on to the misunderstandings that had taken place in this stage of my life. I was holding on the the failures that captured me at this stage of my life. I was holding on to the mental emotions that flooded my mind in this stage of my life. All along self-forgiveness had not taken place because I hadn't allowed it to take place.

Why was this such a hard stage of my life???

Why was forgiving myself so hard for me to do?

Was it that I came to a position in my life where I felt like I did not deserve forgiveness?

In my mindset I always ask…..

Why did I deserve forgiveness when I turned around and did what leadership told me not to do. I brought this stage of my life upon myself, so why did I deserve forgiveness…

This was not just about self-forgiveness, this was about forgiveness in general. I was beginning to truly understand that unforgiveness will leave you burdened down. Unforgiveness will cause you to start living your life in bondage. I knew in my heart that I did not want to live my life in bondage! Thats basically handing your life over to the enemy, and I knew for sure that I had so much more fight within me! Once you allow bondage to take over, bondage then becomes a form of depression. Depression will then bring about thoughts of non-existence in life. Because I did not allow unforgiveness to take place in the beginning, my mindset took another route and I wanted to end my own life. I quickly caught on to the realization that unforgiveness was only hindering my healing process. Keep in mind, you do not want anything to hinder your healing process.

It was time!

It was time to confront the person that lived within me. The person that felt as if she was worthless. The person that felt as if no man would ever want her again. The person that felt as if she did not deserve another chance. The person that felt as if she placed a man before God. The person that felt as if she failed life. The person that felt as if she no longer had a purpose. The person that felt as if she had nothing else to give. I begin to forgive that person that meant the most to me in life and that person was "Me". This had become one of the major aspects in my life to begin my healing process and returning home from Mississippi.

I must say that returning home I was a bit lost, wasn't sure on where to start the rebuilding process. I had to make decisions that were best for Lorinda. The first thing I had to do was to begin forgiving myself! Once again I was stuck. I did not know how to forgive myself! I did not know where to begin! My life was a mess! I didn't know how to deal with the feelings that I had captured within myself. What does it really mean to heal? What does it really mean to give yourself time to rebuild? What does it really mean to set yourself aside to allow God to use you? I was broken, I needed God to put me back together again!!! In order for God to do what he needed to do I had to surrender all to him! I had to turn my life completely over to him. That means I had to stop trying to fix things on my own. I had to stop searching for love when I didn't completely love myself. I had to stop blaming my husband for a broken marriage and take some responsibility upon myself. Again the biggest thing that had to take place was forgiveness within myself.

Did I feel like I deserve God's forgiveness??? In my opinion no I did not because I brought all of this upon myself. But this is why God is God, and everyday he gives us Grace and Mercy to start over again! God's Grace and Mercy covers us when we are out of his boundaries!!! Even though I had placed my life in unknown territory, God's grace and mercy had continued to cover me. Through it all, His grace and mercy covered me. Even when I attempted to take myself out of this world God's grace and mercy covered me.

The nights where I cried alone begging for my husband to lie beside me, God's Grace and Mercy covered me. The evenings where I walked the Gulf Coast of Mississippi just wanting to jump into the water and sink God's Grace and Mercy covered me. The nights where I got into my car and drove for hours just wanting to get away, God's Grace and Mercy covered me! This only shows me that I can begin to forgive myself because God's Grace and Mercy covered me!!!

Chapter 8
Spiritually Under Construction

It was time for me to back track and pick up all the missing pieces from my life that I had dropped along the way. Here they were in my hands the pieces of my life and I did not know what to do with them. All I could do was hand them over to God. I lied there spiritually and allowed God to put me back together again piece by piece. Everything about my mind, body, soul and spirit had to be lined up with the word of God. It was time that I commanded my life to fall in line with the word of God. Needless to say, this was a process. A process that was going to take some time. In this time frame I had to learn to be still and allow God to work. I had to learn to be still and confirm the voice of God. I had to learn to be still and welcome the voice of God back into my life. I had to learn to be still and welcome the Holy Spirit back into myself.

At that moment, I felt myself connecting to God again, I began hearing the voice of God again! I received from God these 4 words over and over agin into my spirit "You belong to me"!!! I began repeating that over and over again in my spirit, "I belong to God, I belong to God, I belong to God, I belong to God, I belong to God"… The more and more it flooded through my vocal cords that more my heart and soul began to accept it. It finally clicked that despite what I had gone through, despite how I how felt, despite where I've gone, despite what I had given up, despite what I had lost, despite what the results were, God still says I belong to him.

God was there with his arms opened waiting for me to return to him. I failed to realized that when I married this man, I had given up on God.

When returning home, my biggest fear was facing everyone, while also accepting and receiving all that had to be said. There was nothing in this world to prepare me for the words that were spit out of the mouths of others. All the "I told you so's" that I received! If I got $10 for ever "I told you so" I received I would be rich on today! But then something hit my spirit! If I had begun to forgive myself first like God instructed me to do, accepting the words of others would have been easier for me to receive. Once the forgiveness of the self began, I was able to face anyone and say, "Yes my marriage failed"& "Yes I'm still standing"... speaking those words gave me strength within itself!

Why did I care so much about what my family and friends were going it say. I'm sure it was only out of love, but at the same time hearing the same things over and over again, you will begin blaming yourself again, and your right back in the place you started. I had to make a decision. Either I was going to continue to entertain what others were saying to me or I was truly there to allow God to rebuild my life again. Was I going to allow people to keep pushing me to explain and make since of what took place in my past? Or was I actually going to forgive myself and move forward? I had gotten to a point to where I understood that no one can make these decisions for me! But here's the problem that I carried... why did the opinion of others mattered so much to me? I think it was because I felt as if when I return home I had to convince myself and others that they were right about me making the biggest mistake of my life. This had became such a sensitive area of my life that I decided to just shut down. Eventually people stop interrogating me and they begin to truly help me.

There were those who truly took me by the hand and helped me make Illinois my home once again. First of foremost it was time to acknowledge the level of attention that my life needed. I had to make it very clear to God that I was ready to be made over again. I was ready for the rebuilding process. After getting married I found myself giving my all to an individual. I emptied myself out! I didn't seem to be myself anymore. Things became cloudy even whenI was trying to seek for help I could not spiritually see. This was truly me that I'm explaining. So I had to ask God to come in and truly rebuild within me. My mind, body and soul! Every part of me. I could not hold anything back in order for God to do his work!!! Therefore at this point of my life my body became spiritually under construction!

Chapter 9
Re-Acceptance

God needed to get to my spirit in order to begin this re-acceptance process within me. This means that I had do be opened and dissected spiritually. When you've been broken so deeply you have to get to the cord to begin the healing process. My spirit became weak and it caused my body to respond in a weak way. God sat me down one day and asked me, "what part do I play in my healing process"? It took me a while to truly understand what God had asked me. "What did he mean what part did I played in my healing process???"

God... please break this down for me because I am not understanding what you are meaning. All I continued to hear in my spirit for about two days was " What part do you play in your healing process"!!! Finally my spirit connected to the question God continued to ask me for days! My part in my healing process was to "release"!!! Seems so simple right!!!! But it wasn't that simply. I had to truly release everything! Everything from the beginning to end not holding anything back. With the help of God I leveled up with myself and accepted the fact that I needed spiritual counseling while trying to heal. I've learned that each individual that decide to choose counseling will respond to counseling spiritually in a different way.

Mentally I was not responding to counseling, my mental state was not reacting to what was provided in counseling. In my heart I truly believe that the mental part of me became very fragile. Every other day I had a breakdown. Was it ok for me to be so fragile allow God to use me? How was God able to use me if I was so fragile? Be mentally fragile it was so easy for me to lose sight of God again. It was easy for me to lose focus of what God was wanting from me. In this fragile stage of my life I had to be very careful of who I surround myself with. It was time that I actually made my way back to the house of God. At this point I had to truly gather myself because it was time that I can knowledge that I had to face my spiritual parents and my church family.

It hurt me deeply because I knew at the end of the day they were right and I was wrong. I had to truly accept the fact that I was walking in disobedience. My spiritual parents were my Pastors Andrea and Arthur who helped mold my life back into place. Throughout everything I have been through in life they've continued to have my best interest at heart. I can remember the day my spiritual pants sat me down on the couch in their home. The words that flowed out of their mouths hit heart because I knew everything that was spoken happened to be true. It was so hard because when the enemy has your mind captured in his hand, anything anyone had to say became so foggy in my spirit.

My ears became closed to the truth. After everything that was spoken my spirit was stuck in the mist of decisions that had been made without God! Failing to realize at the moment that decisions that are made without God will be failures in the long run. My pastors sent me down as their own child and spoke to me directly on this decision of getting married. After everything that had already taken place in my life they knew as well as I knew that I was not ready to be married. I remember leaving their home after talking with them and I pulled up into my parking lot. I sat in my car and I cried and cried as tears tears fell from my face I knew in my heart that I had no business marrying this man.

We were not spiritually on the same page. We were not spiritually connected what so ever. Those again with the two biggest red flags that I happened to miss. I must say that I was truly afraid to face my spiritual parents once returning home from Mississippi. I felt as if I did not deserve to be a member of the church anymore. So regretting the fact that I had to face them I began attending other churches. For some odd reason each Sunday that I'd decided to attend a church that was not my own my soul remain lost. Deep down in my spirit I knew where I should have been. It was time that I faced reality. If I actually wanted healing to take place in my spirit I needed to go back to my foundation and place of healing. Days and weeks had passed, my soul was getting sicker and sicker! I needed my spiritual parents!!! I can remember the Sunday my heart was hurting long enough.

I had finally decided to return to my church home after being back from Mississippi for some time. As I sat in the service I could not seem to get into the word that was spoken. I felt a little out of place after not being there for so long. I felt like a runaway! I then felt as if I owed everyone and I mean everyone in my church family an apology. After being there the feeling became real that I did not deserve to be there. As Bishop continued to speak through his message my heart had begun to unfold. I can remember a quote he stated in his message on this Sunday! And once he said it, it was confirmation that I needed to get it together!!! He stated to " To never put yourself in position to be tempted by the enemy"... When Pastor stayed that, things began to make sense. That one quote from the mouth of my Bishop made me spiritually connected once again!

This same Sunday after the word was spoken, my Pastors called me to the alter and wrapped their arms around me. I can remember weeping and weeping on my Co-Pastors shoulder. I wrapped my arms around her and I didn't want to let her go. Despite what took place in my life, despite the decisions I had made, despite the mistakes I had made that lead to my departure, my spiritual parents and my church family welcomed me back with opened arms. They loved on me like never before. I was back connected with my family, and "My God"…..was this literally the best day of my life. Being in the presence of individuals that did not judge me but helped me to get back on the right track was the most amazing feeling ever.

Needless to say, without this connection with my spiritual family I was truly lost I had no sense of direction no understanding no spiritual vision no connection with myself whatsoever, I truly needed not only my spiritual parents but my spiritual family as well. Being back home spiritually, and being back connected to where God sent me, it then hit that this is where now forgiving myself my come into play!

Chapter 10
Final Destination

I had to begin forgiving myself and allowing God to get me to a stage in my life where He can use me. Now don't get me wrong it was yet very very difficult for me to truly accept that I had to allow God to make me over. This wasn't the final destination of my life that God needed me to be. Not only did I have to divorce this man, I also had to divorce everything that was not of God from my life. If it wasn't in the plan of God I had to divorce it. If it drew my attention off God I had to divorce it. If it took me off the path that God had directed me on I had to divorce it. If it kept me from being in the house of God I had to divorce it.

I had to mentally, physically and spiritually divorce any and everything that had me disconnected from God. I had to get to the final destination that God needed me to be in order to beginning healing. My biggest thing I had to begin doing was loving myself. I had to love myself enough to say that I deserved more. I had to love myself enough to say that I deserved better. I had to love myself to know and believe that I was a child of child and He loves me. I had became so disconnected from God to where I wasn't sure if I would ever be able to hear from God again. The hardest thing I had to get through was truly asking God to forgive me for attempting to end my own life.

When things get to a point to where they make you want to end your own life, it was basically saying that I believe that this was something that God could not pull me through. I allowed a worldly attraction to create in me a deaf ear toward the voice of God. Ending my life on my own would not have gotten me to the final destination that God had landscaped out for me. When the thought of suicide creates a place in the mindset, you begin to give up on everything and everyone. Once brought back to a stable state in the hospital after trying to commit suicide it truly hit my spirit deeply that God had just given me another chance on life. God gave me another chance to be the person he created me to be.

God gave me another chance to start over. God gave me another chance to trust him. God gave me another chance to put my past behind me. God gave me another chance to use my voice to tell my testimony. God gave me another chance to make it to my final destination. It was up to me to try to push forward! Here before me I had a clean slate. At the same time it took me a while to accept this new beginning. I felt undeserving! For a long time I hated myself, I most of all hated the mistakes that I allowed to take part of my life.

The enemy truly had me believing that I did not deserve another chance from God. As days and months began to past God revealed to me that he was truly a forgiving God!!! It was up to me to begin walking in my forgiveness. I had to deeply realize that God's forgiveness was the ultimate forgiveness that would get me to my feet again. When God's forgiveness takes place, life begins to feel worth living again. God extended his grace and mercy over my life. All there was left for me to do is accept and have faith! So the real question was, where do I go from here???

All that was left to do was go forward! This was my life and I had to take control of every aspect that took place. I was accountable for what happened from this point on. Everything that had taken place in my life previously and anything involving the failed marriage God had it expunged from my record! The only way it could be brought back up is if I allowed the enemy to take over my life again, and with God's Grace & Mercy that was not going to happen!

End "Reflections"...

When getting married, God does not want you to forget who you are as a person. Yes, when intwining your life with someone else's life, the two of you become one mentally, physically and spiritually, but it is important that you remember who you are and who God has called you to be. Remembering who you are and remembering who God is will help you to understand what God's plan is within your life. When God brings two souls together, he will connect you with someone that will help you to grow in every aspect of your life. God will never connect you with someone that will belittle you, look down on you, or use you as a cover up. God will never connect you with someone through marriage that will "MUTE" you.

You have a voice, speak what's right. Teach what's right. Marriage should never cause an individual to change in a bad way. Marriage should never place you in a category of wanting to give up on life. Marriage is a commitment that should be shared between two, which you should never be in the commitment alone. Two individuals connected together through God mentally, physically and spiritually are said to be equally yoked. God will "NEVER" connect you with someone that isn't equally yoked with you mentally, physically and most of all spiritually!

Reflection Journal

Throughout the process of constructing my life back together I kept a journal. There were moments within this stage of my life where I was afraid to reach out and talk to someone because I feared I would be judged, talked about or even shamed. I decided that I would just write unto God. I knew that He would listen to me and comfort me. Ive decided to attach a journal at the end of this book. Moments that you may feel as if your not physically able to talk with someone, feel free to write in this journal.

Always remember that God is listening...

Date: _____

Dear God today I am most grateful for.....

_____
_____
_____
_____
_____
_____
_____
_____
_____
_____
_____
_____
_____
_____
_____
_____
_____
_____
_____

Date: _____

Dear God today I am most grateful for......

_____
_____
_____
_____
_____
_____
_____
_____
_____
_____
_____
_____
_____
_____
_____
_____
_____

Date: _____

Dear God today I am most grateful for……

_____
_____
_____
_____
_____
_____
_____
_____
_____
_____
_____
_____
_____
_____
_____
_____
_____
_____
_____

Date: _____

Dear God today I am most grateful for.....

Date: _____

Dear God today I am most grateful for.....

_____
_____
_____
_____
_____
_____
_____
_____
_____
_____
_____
_____
_____
_____
_____
_____
_____
_____
_____
_____

Date: _____

Dear God today I am most grateful for.....

_____
_____
_____
_____
_____
_____
_____
_____
_____
_____
_____
_____
_____
_____
_____
_____
_____

Date: _____

Dear God today I am most grateful for......

_____
_____
_____
_____
_____
_____
_____
_____
_____
_____
_____
_____
_____
_____
_____
_____
_____
_____

Date: _____

Dear God today I am most grateful for.....

_____
_____
_____
_____
_____
_____
_____
_____
_____
_____
_____
_____
_____
_____
_____
_____
_____
_____
_____

Date: _____

Dear God today I am most grateful for.....

Date: _____

Dear God today I am most grateful for.....

_____
_____
_____
_____
_____
_____
_____
_____
_____
_____
_____
_____
_____
_____
_____
_____
_____

Date: _____

Dear God today I am most grateful for.....

_____
_____
_____
_____
_____
_____
_____
_____
_____
_____
_____
_____
_____
_____
_____
_____
_____
_____
_____

Date: _____

Dear God today I am most grateful for.....

_____
_____
_____
_____
_____
_____
_____
_____
_____
_____
_____
_____
_____
_____
_____
_____
_____
_____

Date: _____

Dear God today I am most grateful for......

_____
_____
_____
_____
_____
_____
_____
_____
_____
_____
_____
_____
_____
_____
_____
_____
_____

Date: _____

Dear God today I am most grateful for.....

_____
_____
_____
_____
_____
_____
_____
_____
_____
_____
_____
_____
_____
_____
_____
_____
_____

Date: _____

Dear God today I am most grateful for.....

_____
_____
_____
_____
_____
_____
_____
_____
_____
_____
_____
_____
_____
_____
_____
_____
_____
_____
_____
_____

Date: _____

Dear God today I am most grateful for.....

Date: _____

Dear God today I am most grateful for……

Date: _____

Dear God today I am most grateful for.....

_____
_____
_____
_____
_____
_____
_____
_____
_____
_____
_____
_____
_____
_____
_____
_____
_____
_____
_____

Date: _____

Dear God today I am most grateful for......

_____
_____
_____
_____
_____
_____
_____
_____
_____
_____
_____
_____
_____
_____
_____
_____
_____
_____

Date: _____

Dear God today I am most grateful for…..

_____
_____
_____
_____
_____
_____
_____
_____
_____
_____
_____
_____
_____
_____
_____
_____
_____
_____
_____
_____

Date: _____

Dear God today I am most grateful for.....

Date: _____

Dear God today I am most grateful for......

Date: _____

Dear God today I am most grateful for.....

_____
_____
_____
_____
_____
_____
_____
_____
_____
_____
_____
_____
_____
_____
_____
_____
_____
_____
_____

Date: _____

Dear God today I am most grateful for.....

_____
_____
_____
_____
_____
_____
_____
_____
_____
_____
_____
_____
_____
_____
_____
_____
_____

Date: _____

Dear God today I am most grateful for.....

_____
_____
_____
_____
_____
_____
_____
_____
_____
_____
_____
_____
_____
_____
_____
_____

Date: _____

Dear God today I am most grateful for…..

_____
_____
_____
_____
_____
_____
_____
_____
_____
_____
_____
_____
_____
_____
_____
_____
_____
_____

Date: _____

Dear God today I am most grateful for.....

_____
_____
_____
_____
_____
_____
_____
_____
_____
_____
_____
_____
_____
_____
_____
_____
_____

Date: _____

Dear God today I am most grateful for.....

Date: _____

Dear God today I am most grateful for......

_____
_____
_____
_____
_____
_____
_____
_____
_____
_____
_____
_____
_____
_____
_____
_____
_____
_____
_____

Date: _____

Dear God today I am most grateful for......

_____
_____
_____
_____
_____
_____
_____
_____
_____
_____
_____
_____
_____
_____
_____
_____
_____

Date: _____

Dear God today I am most grateful for......

_____
_____
_____
_____
_____
_____
_____
_____
_____
_____
_____
_____
_____
_____
_____
_____
_____
_____
_____
_____

Date: _____

Dear God today I am most grateful for.....

_____
_____
_____
_____
_____
_____
_____
_____
_____
_____
_____
_____
_____
_____
_____
_____
_____
_____
_____
_____
_____

Date: _____

Dear God today I am most grateful for......

_____
_____
_____
_____
_____
_____
_____
_____
_____
_____
_____
_____
_____
_____
_____
_____
_____
_____
_____

Date: _____

Dear God today I am most grateful for.....

_____
_____
_____
_____
_____
_____
_____
_____
_____
_____
_____
_____
_____
_____
_____
_____
_____
_____
_____

Date: _____

Dear God today I am most grateful for.....

_____
_____
_____
_____
_____
_____
_____
_____
_____
_____
_____
_____
_____
_____
_____
_____
_____
_____
_____
_____

Date: _____

Dear God today I am most grateful for.....

_____
_____
_____
_____
_____
_____
_____
_____
_____
_____
_____
_____
_____
_____
_____
_____
_____
_____
_____
_____

Date: _____

Dear God today I am most grateful for.....

_____
_____
_____
_____
_____
_____
_____
_____
_____
_____
_____
_____
_____
_____
_____
_____
_____
_____
_____
_____

Date: _____

Dear God today I am most grateful for......

_____
_____
_____
_____
_____
_____
_____
_____
_____
_____
_____
_____
_____
_____
_____
_____
_____
_____
_____
_____

Date: _____

Dear God today I am most grateful for.....

_____
_____
_____
_____
_____
_____
_____
_____
_____
_____
_____
_____
_____
_____
_____
_____
_____
_____
_____
_____

Date: _____

Dear God today I am most grateful for……

_____
_____
_____
_____
_____
_____
_____
_____
_____
_____
_____
_____
_____
_____
_____
_____
_____
_____
_____
_____
_____

Date: _____

Dear God today I am most grateful for.....

Date: _____

Dear God today I am most grateful for......

_____
_____
_____
_____
_____
_____
_____
_____
_____
_____
_____
_____
_____
_____
_____
_____
_____
_____
_____

Date: _____

Dear God today I am most grateful for......

_____
_____
_____
_____
_____
_____
_____
_____
_____
_____
_____
_____
_____
_____
_____
_____
_____

Date: _____

Dear God today I am most grateful for.....

Date: _____

Dear God today I am most grateful for.....

Date: _____

Dear God today I am most grateful for.....

_____
_____
_____
_____
_____
_____
_____
_____
_____
_____
_____
_____
_____
_____
_____
_____
_____
_____
_____
_____

Date: _____

Dear God today I am most grateful for.....

_____
_____
_____
_____
_____
_____
_____
_____
_____
_____
_____
_____
_____
_____
_____
_____
_____
_____

Date: _____

Dear God today I am most grateful for......

_____
_____
_____
_____
_____
_____
_____
_____
_____
_____
_____
_____
_____
_____
_____
_____
_____
_____
_____
_____

Date: _____

Dear God today I am most grateful for.....

Date: _____

Dear God today I am most grateful for.....

_____
_____
_____
_____
_____
_____
_____
_____
_____
_____
_____
_____
_____
_____
_____
_____
_____
_____
_____

Date: _____

Dear God today I am most grateful for.....

Date: _____

Dear God today I am most grateful for…..

_____
_____
_____
_____
_____
_____
_____
_____
_____
_____
_____
_____
_____
_____
_____
_____
_____
_____

Date: _____

Dear God today I am most grateful for.....

_____
_____
_____
_____
_____
_____
_____
_____
_____
_____
_____
_____
_____
_____
_____
_____
_____
_____
_____

Date: _____

Dear God today I am most grateful for.....

_____
_____
_____
_____
_____
_____
_____
_____
_____
_____
_____
_____
_____
_____
_____
_____
_____
_____
_____
_____

Date: _____

Dear God today I am most grateful for.....

Date: _____

Dear God today I am most grateful for.....

_____
_____
_____
_____
_____
_____
_____
_____
_____
_____
_____
_____
_____
_____
_____
_____
_____
_____
_____
_____
_____

Date: _____

Dear God today I am most grateful for…..

Date: _____

Dear God today I am most grateful for......

_____
_____
_____
_____
_____
_____
_____
_____
_____
_____
_____
_____
_____
_____
_____
_____
_____
_____

Date: _____

Dear God today I am most grateful for.....

Date: _____

Dear God today I am most grateful for……

_____
_____
_____
_____
_____
_____
_____
_____
_____
_____
_____
_____
_____
_____
_____
_____
_____
_____
_____
_____

Date: _____

Dear God today I am most grateful for......

_____
_____
_____
_____
_____
_____
_____
_____
_____
_____
_____
_____
_____
_____
_____
_____
_____
_____
_____
_____

Date: _____

Dear God today I am most grateful for…..

_____
_____
_____
_____
_____
_____
_____
_____
_____
_____
_____
_____
_____
_____
_____
_____
_____
_____
_____
_____

Date: _____

Dear God today I am most grateful for.....

_____
_____
_____
_____
_____
_____
_____
_____
_____
_____
_____
_____
_____
_____
_____
_____
_____
_____
_____
_____

Date: _____

Dear God today I am most grateful for......

_____
_____
_____
_____
_____
_____
_____
_____
_____
_____
_____
_____
_____
_____
_____
_____
_____
_____
_____
_____

Date: _____

Dear God today I am most grateful for.....

_____
_____
_____
_____
_____
_____
_____
_____
_____
_____
_____
_____
_____
_____
_____
_____
_____
_____
_____

Date: _____

Dear God today I am most grateful for.....

Date: _____

Dear God today I am most grateful for......

_____
_____
_____
_____
_____
_____
_____
_____
_____
_____
_____
_____
_____
_____
_____
_____
_____
_____
_____
_____

Date: _____

Dear God today I am most grateful for......

_____
_____
_____
_____
_____
_____
_____
_____
_____
_____
_____
_____
_____
_____
_____
_____
_____
_____
_____

Date: _____

Dear God today I am most grateful for......

Date: _____

Dear God today I am most grateful for.....

Date: _____

Dear God today I am most grateful for.....

Date: _____

Dear God today I am most grateful for......

_____
_____
_____
_____
_____
_____
_____
_____
_____
_____
_____
_____
_____
_____
_____
_____
_____
_____
_____

Date: _____

Dear God today I am most grateful for.....

_____
_____
_____
_____
_____
_____
_____
_____
_____
_____
_____
_____
_____
_____
_____
_____
_____
_____
_____
_____

Date: _____

Dear God today I am most grateful for……

Date: _____

Dear God today I am most grateful for.....

Date: _____

Dear God today I am most grateful for......

_____
_____
_____
_____
_____
_____
_____
_____
_____
_____
_____
_____
_____
_____
_____
_____
_____
_____
_____

Date: _____

Dear God today I am most grateful for......

_____
_____
_____
_____
_____
_____
_____
_____
_____
_____
_____
_____
_____
_____
_____
_____
_____
_____
_____

Date: _____

Dear God today I am most grateful for......

_____
_____
_____
_____
_____
_____
_____
_____
_____
_____
_____
_____
_____
_____
_____
_____
_____
_____

Date: _____

Dear God today I am most grateful for......

_____
_____
_____
_____
_____
_____
_____
_____
_____
_____
_____
_____
_____
_____
_____
_____
_____
_____

Date: _____

Dear God today I am most grateful for.....

_____
_____
_____
_____
_____
_____
_____
_____
_____
_____
_____
_____
_____
_____
_____
_____
_____
_____
_____
_____
_____
_____
_____
_____

Date: _____

Dear God today I am most grateful for.....

_____
_____
_____
_____
_____
_____
_____
_____
_____
_____
_____
_____
_____
_____
_____
_____
_____
_____
_____
_____

Date: _____

Dear God today I am most grateful for……

_____
_____
_____
_____
_____
_____
_____
_____
_____
_____
_____
_____
_____
_____
_____
_____
_____
_____
_____

Date: _____

Dear God today I am most grateful for......

_____
_____
_____
_____
_____
_____
_____
_____
_____
_____
_____
_____
_____
_____
_____
_____
_____
_____
_____
_____

Date: _____

Dear God today I am most grateful for......

_____
_____
_____
_____
_____
_____
_____
_____
_____
_____
_____
_____
_____
_____
_____
_____
_____
_____
_____
_____
_____

Date: _____

Dear God today I am most grateful for.....

Date: _____

Dear God today I am most grateful for......

Date: _____

Dear God today I am most grateful for.....

_____
_____
_____
_____
_____
_____
_____
_____
_____
_____
_____
_____
_____
_____
_____
_____
_____
_____
_____
_____

Date: _____

Dear God today I am most grateful for.....

Date: _____

Dear God today I am most grateful for.....

Date: _____

Dear God today I am most grateful for.....

Date: _____

Dear God today I am most grateful for.....

Date: _____

Dear God today I am most grateful for......

_____
_____
_____
_____
_____
_____
_____
_____
_____
_____
_____
_____
_____
_____
_____
_____
_____
_____
_____
_____

Date: _____

Dear God today I am most grateful for.....

Date: _____

Dear God today I am most grateful for......

Date: _____

Dear God today I am most grateful for.....

Date: _____

Dear God today I am most grateful for.....

_____
_____
_____
_____
_____
_____
_____
_____
_____
_____
_____
_____
_____
_____
_____
_____

Date: _____

Dear God today I am most grateful for.....

_____
_____
_____
_____
_____
_____
_____
_____
_____
_____
_____
_____
_____
_____
_____
_____
_____
_____

Date: _____

Dear God today I am most grateful for.....

Date: _____

Dear God today I am most grateful for.....

Date: _____

Dear God today I am most grateful for.....

Date: _____

Dear God today I am most grateful for.....

_____
_____
_____
_____
_____
_____
_____
_____
_____
_____
_____
_____
_____
_____
_____
_____
_____
_____
_____
_____
_____

Date: _____

Dear God today I am most grateful for.....

_____
_____
_____
_____
_____
_____
_____
_____
_____
_____
_____
_____
_____
_____
_____
_____
_____
_____
_____
_____

Date: _____

Dear God today I am most grateful for…..

Date: _____

Dear God today I am most grateful for.....

Date: _____

Dear God today I am most grateful for......

_____
_____
_____
_____
_____
_____
_____
_____
_____
_____
_____
_____
_____
_____
_____
_____
_____
_____
_____
_____

Date: _____

Dear God today I am most grateful for.....

Date: _____

Dear God today I am most grateful for.....

_____
_____
_____
_____
_____
_____
_____
_____
_____
_____
_____
_____
_____
_____
_____
_____
_____
_____
_____
_____
_____

Date: _____

Dear God today I am most grateful for.....

_____
_____
_____
_____
_____
_____
_____
_____
_____
_____
_____
_____
_____
_____
_____
_____
_____
_____
_____
_____

Date: _____

Dear God today I am most grateful for......

_____
_____
_____
_____
_____
_____
_____
_____
_____
_____
_____
_____
_____
_____
_____
_____
_____

Date: _____

Dear God today I am most grateful for......

Date: _____

Dear God today I am most grateful for......

_____
_____
_____
_____
_____
_____
_____
_____
_____
_____
_____
_____
_____
_____
_____
_____
_____
_____
_____
_____

Date: _____

Dear God today I am most grateful for.....

_____
_____
_____
_____
_____
_____
_____
_____
_____
_____
_____
_____
_____
_____
_____
_____
_____
_____
_____
_____

Date: _____

Dear God today I am most grateful for.....

_____
_____
_____
_____
_____
_____
_____
_____
_____
_____
_____
_____
_____
_____
_____
_____
_____
_____
_____
_____

Date: _____

Dear God today I am most grateful for……

Date: _____

Dear God today I am most grateful for......

_____
_____
_____
_____
_____
_____
_____
_____
_____
_____
_____
_____
_____
_____
_____
_____
_____
_____
_____
_____

Date: _____

Dear God today I am most grateful for……

_____
_____
_____
_____
_____
_____
_____
_____
_____
_____
_____
_____
_____
_____
_____
_____
_____
_____
_____
_____

Date: _____

Dear God today I am most grateful for.....

_____
_____
_____
_____
_____
_____
_____
_____
_____
_____
_____
_____
_____
_____
_____
_____
_____
_____

Date: _____

Dear God today I am most grateful for......

_____
_____
_____
_____
_____
_____
_____
_____
_____
_____
_____
_____
_____
_____
_____
_____
_____
_____
_____

Date: _____

Dear God today I am most grateful for.....

_____
_____
_____
_____
_____
_____
_____
_____
_____
_____
_____
_____
_____
_____
_____
_____
_____
_____
_____
_____

Date: _____

Dear God today I am most grateful for......

_____
_____
_____
_____
_____
_____
_____
_____
_____
_____
_____
_____
_____
_____
_____
_____
_____
_____

Date: _____

Dear God today I am most grateful for…..

Date: _____

Dear God today I am most grateful for.....

Date: _____

Dear God today I am most grateful for.....

_____
_____
_____
_____
_____
_____
_____
_____
_____
_____
_____
_____
_____
_____
_____
_____
_____
_____
_____
_____

Date: _____

Dear God today I am most grateful for.....

Date: _____

Dear God today I am most grateful for.....

Date: _____

Dear God today I am most grateful for......

Date: _____

Dear God today I am most grateful for......

Date: _____

Dear God today I am most grateful for......

Date: _____

Dear God today I am most grateful for.....

_____
_____
_____
_____
_____
_____
_____
_____
_____
_____
_____
_____
_____
_____
_____
_____
_____
_____
_____
_____

Date: _____

Dear God today I am most grateful for......

_____
_____
_____
_____
_____
_____
_____
_____
_____
_____
_____
_____
_____
_____
_____
_____
_____
_____

Date: _____

Dear God today I am most grateful for.....

Date: _____

Dear God today I am most grateful for.....

Date: _____

Dear God today I am most grateful for......

_____
_____
_____
_____
_____
_____
_____
_____
_____
_____
_____
_____
_____
_____
_____
_____
_____
_____
_____

Date: _____

Dear God today I am most grateful for.....

Date: _____

Dear God today I am most grateful for.....

_____
_____
_____
_____
_____
_____
_____
_____
_____
_____
_____
_____
_____
_____
_____
_____
_____
_____

Date: _____

Dear God today I am most grateful for......

Date: _____

Dear God today I am most grateful for…..

_____
_____
_____
_____
_____
_____
_____
_____
_____
_____
_____
_____
_____
_____
_____
_____
_____
_____
_____
_____

Date: _____

Dear God today I am most grateful for.....

_____
_____
_____
_____
_____
_____
_____
_____
_____
_____
_____
_____
_____
_____
_____
_____
_____
_____
_____

Date: _____

Dear God today I am most grateful for......

Date: _____

Dear God today I am most grateful for......

_____
_____
_____
_____
_____
_____
_____
_____
_____
_____
_____
_____
_____
_____
_____
_____
_____
_____
_____

Date: _____

Dear God today I am most grateful for......

_____
_____
_____
_____
_____
_____
_____
_____
_____
_____
_____
_____
_____
_____
_____
_____
_____
_____
_____
_____
_____

Date: _____

Dear God today I am most grateful for.....

Date: _____

Dear God today I am most grateful for.....

_____
_____
_____
_____
_____
_____
_____
_____
_____
_____
_____
_____
_____
_____
_____
_____
_____
_____
_____
_____

Date: _____

Dear God today I am most grateful for.....

Date: _____

Dear God today I am most grateful for.....

Date: _____

Dear God today I am most grateful for.....

Date: _____

Dear God today I am most grateful for......

_____
_____
_____
_____
_____
_____
_____
_____
_____
_____
_____
_____
_____
_____
_____
_____
_____
_____
_____
_____

Date: _____

Dear God today I am most grateful for.....

_____
_____
_____
_____
_____
_____
_____
_____
_____
_____
_____
_____
_____
_____
_____
_____
_____
_____
_____
_____

Date: _____

Dear God today I am most grateful for......

Date: _____

Dear God today I am most grateful for......

Date: _____

Dear God today I am most grateful for......

_____
_____
_____
_____
_____
_____
_____
_____
_____
_____
_____
_____
_____
_____
_____
_____
_____
_____

Date: _____

Dear God today I am most grateful for.....

Date: _____

Dear God today I am most grateful for......

Date: _____

Dear God today I am most grateful for.....

Date: _____

Dear God today I am most grateful for.....

_____
_____
_____
_____
_____
_____
_____
_____
_____
_____
_____
_____
_____
_____
_____
_____
_____
_____

Date: _____

Dear God today I am most grateful for......

Date: _____

Dear God today I am most grateful for……

Date: _____

Dear God today I am most grateful for......

_____
_____
_____
_____
_____
_____
_____
_____
_____
_____
_____
_____
_____
_____
_____
_____
_____
_____
_____

Date: _____

Dear God today I am most grateful for......

Date: _____

Dear God today I am most grateful for.....

_____
_____
_____
_____
_____
_____
_____
_____
_____
_____
_____
_____
_____
_____
_____
_____
_____
_____
_____

Date: _____

Dear God today I am most grateful for.....

_____
_____
_____
_____
_____
_____
_____
_____
_____
_____
_____
_____
_____
_____
_____
_____
_____
_____
_____
_____

Date: _____

Dear God today I am most grateful for.....

_____
_____
_____
_____
_____
_____
_____
_____
_____
_____
_____
_____
_____
_____
_____
_____
_____
_____

Date: _____

Dear God today I am most grateful for.....

_____
_____
_____
_____
_____
_____
_____
_____
_____
_____
_____
_____
_____
_____
_____
_____
_____
_____
_____
_____

Date: _____

Dear God today I am most grateful for......

_____
_____
_____
_____
_____
_____
_____
_____
_____
_____
_____
_____
_____
_____
_____
_____

Date: _____

Dear God today I am most grateful for.....

_____
_____
_____
_____
_____
_____
_____
_____
_____
_____
_____
_____
_____
_____
_____
_____
_____
_____
_____
_____
_____

Date: _____

Dear God today I am most grateful for.....

_____
_____
_____
_____
_____
_____
_____
_____
_____
_____
_____
_____
_____
_____
_____
_____
_____
_____
_____
_____

Date: _____

Dear God today I am most grateful for.....

Date: _____

Dear God today I am most grateful for......

_____
_____
_____
_____
_____
_____
_____
_____
_____
_____
_____
_____
_____
_____
_____
_____
_____
_____
_____
_____
_____

Date: _____

Dear God today I am most grateful for......

_____
_____
_____
_____
_____
_____
_____
_____
_____
_____
_____
_____
_____
_____
_____
_____
_____
_____
_____
_____

Date: _____

Dear God today I am most grateful for......

Date: _____

Dear God today I am most grateful for......

Date: _____

Dear God today I am most grateful for......

Date: _____

Dear God today I am most grateful for.....

_____
_____
_____
_____
_____
_____
_____
_____
_____
_____
_____
_____
_____
_____
_____
_____
_____
_____
_____
_____

Date: _____

Dear God today I am most grateful for......

Date: _____

Dear God today I am most grateful for……

_____
_____
_____
_____
_____
_____
_____
_____
_____
_____
_____
_____
_____
_____
_____
_____
_____
_____
_____

Date: _____

Dear God today I am most grateful for……

Date: _____

Dear God today I am most grateful for.....

Date: _____

Dear God today I am most grateful for.....

Date: _____

Dear God today I am most grateful for.....

Date: _____

Dear God today I am most grateful for.....

_____
_____
_____
_____
_____
_____
_____
_____
_____
_____
_____
_____
_____
_____
_____
_____
_____

Date: _____

Dear God today I am most grateful for......

_____
_____
_____
_____
_____
_____
_____
_____
_____
_____
_____
_____
_____
_____
_____
_____
_____
_____
_____
_____

Date: _____

Dear God today I am most grateful for......

Date: _____

Dear God today I am most grateful for.....

_____
_____
_____
_____
_____
_____
_____
_____
_____
_____
_____
_____
_____
_____
_____
_____
_____
_____
_____
_____
_____
_____

Date: _____

Dear God today I am most grateful for.....

Date: _____

Dear God today I am most grateful for.....

_____
_____
_____
_____
_____
_____
_____
_____
_____
_____
_____
_____
_____
_____
_____
_____
_____
_____
_____
_____

Date: _____

Dear God today I am most grateful for......

Date: _____

Dear God today I am most grateful for……

Date: _____

Dear God today I am most grateful for......

Date: _____

Dear God today I am most grateful for.....

_____
_____
_____
_____
_____
_____
_____
_____
_____
_____
_____
_____
_____
_____
_____
_____
_____

Date: _____

Dear God today I am most grateful for……

Date: _____

Dear God today I am most grateful for.....

_____
_____
_____
_____
_____
_____
_____
_____
_____
_____
_____
_____
_____
_____
_____
_____
_____
_____
_____

Date: _____

Dear God today I am most grateful for.....

_____
_____
_____
_____
_____
_____
_____
_____
_____
_____
_____
_____
_____
_____
_____
_____
_____
_____
_____
_____

Date: _____

Dear God today I am most grateful for.....

_____
_____
_____
_____
_____
_____
_____
_____
_____
_____
_____
_____
_____
_____
_____
_____
_____
_____
_____
_____